INSIDE MLB

ANGELS

BY PATRICK DONNELLY

SportsZone
An Imprint of Abdo Publishing
abdobooks.com

abdobooks.com

Published by Abdo Publishing, a division of ABDO, PO Box 398166, Minneapolis, Minnesota 55439. Copyright © 2023 by Abdo Consulting Group, Inc. International copyrights reserved in all countries. No part of this book may be reproduced in any form without written permission from the publisher. SportsZone™ is a trademark and logo of Abdo Publishing.

Printed in the United States of America, North Mankato, Minnesota.
102022
012023

Cover Photo: Steph Chambers/Getty Images Sport/Getty Images
Interior Photos: Matt Dirksen/Colorado Rockies/Getty Images Sport/Getty Images, 4; Alex Trautwig/Getty Images Sport/Getty Images, 6; Bettmann/Getty Images, 9; Bruce Bennett Studios/Getty Images Studios/Getty Images, 10; Focus on Sport/Getty Images, 12; Mark Avery/AP Images, 16; Focus on Sport/Getty Images Sport/Getty Images, 17, 18, 21, 22; Owen C. Shaw/Getty Images Sport/Getty Images, 19; Dave Tenenbaum/AP Images, 25; John Cordes/Icon Sportswire/AP Images, 27, 32; Larry Goren/Four Seam Images/AP Images, 28; Jeff Haynes/AFP/Getty Images, 30, 31; David Hood/Cal Sport Media/AP Images, 35; Mark J. Terrill/AP Images, 36; Master Press/Getty Images Sport/Getty Images, 39; Ronald Martinez/Getty Images Sport/Getty Images, 40

Editor: Charlie Beattie
Series Designer: Becky Daum

Library of Congress Control Number: 2022940498

Publisher's Cataloging-in-Publication Data

Names: Donnelly, Patrick, author.
Title: Los Angeles Angels / by Patrick Donnelly
Description: Minneapolis, Minnesota: Abdo Publishing, 2023 | Series: Inside MLB | Includes online resources and index.
Identifiers: ISBN 9781098290207 (lib. bdg.) | ISBN 9781098275402 (ebook)
Subjects: LCSH: Los Angeles Angels (Baseball team)--Juvenile literature. | Baseball teams--Juvenile literature. | Professional sports--Juvenile literature. | Sports franchises--Juvenile literature. | Major League Baseball (Organization)--Juvenile literature.
Classification: DDC 796.35764--dc23

CONTENTS

CHAPTER 1
SHO-TIME 4

CHAPTER 2
PLAYOFFS AND PAIN 12

CHAPTER 3
AT LONG LAST 22

CHAPTER 4
LEGENDARY TEAMMATES 32

TIMELINE 42
TEAM FACTS 44
TEAM TRIVIA 45
GLOSSARY 46
MORE INFORMATION 47
ONLINE RESOURCES 47
INDEX 48
ABOUT THE AUTHOR 48

CHAPTER 1

SHO-TIME

As Shohei Ohtani walked to the mound at Denver's Coors Field, he wasn't looking to make history. But a player with his skills can't help but set a few records along the way.

The 2021 Major League Baseball (MLB) All-Star Game was the 91st in league history. It also proved to be a perfect showcase for the game's most unique talent.

The baseball world hadn't seen a player like Ohtani since the days of Babe Ruth. It's rare to find an outstanding pitcher who's also one of the best hitters in the game. But like Ruth, Ohtani was the whole package.

Ohtani delivers a pitch at the 2021 MLB All-Star Game in Denver, Colorado.

He had already displayed his amazing power at the plate the night before at the annual Home Run Derby. There, he set a record with six home runs that traveled at least 500 feet. Now Ohtani was the starting pitcher and designated hitter for the American League (AL) team. He led off the game by hitting a sharp ground ball that nearly got through the infield. It took a nice play by the second baseman to get him out.

Still, the night's biggest moment was yet to come. When he threw his first pitch to National League (NL) leadoff hitter Fernando Tatís Jr., Ohtani became the first player to bat leadoff and pitch in an All-Star Game. He retired the three NL batters he faced on a high fly ball and two routine grounders. Two of his pitches topped 100 miles per hour (161 km/h).

"It has to amaze everybody," Tatís later said. "If people ever wondered and wanted to see the legend of Babe Ruth, this guy is going the same way and on the same path. Hopefully, he can be healthy, and he can keep it going. It's great for the game."

GO WEST

Big names and legendary feats are nothing new in Los Angeles. The center of the entertainment industry has been home to movie stars, rock stars, and TV stars for decades. But it wasn't always home to star athletes.

Most American professional sports leagues began play with teams centered on the country's East Coast. For a long time, that's where the biggest cities such as New York, Boston, and Washington, DC, were found. But as more and more Americans moved west during the early 1900s, the population of West Coast cities boomed. Major league sports took notice, and soon they arrived on the West Coast too.

Baseball followed that pattern. Before 1958 no MLB team had ever been located west of St. Louis. Then the owners of the Brooklyn Dodgers and New York Giants decided to leave New York City for California. They landed in Los Angeles and San Francisco, respectively. Both cities greeted their new teams warmly. The Dodgers and the Giants saw huge rises in attendance.

In 1961 the AL was expanding by two teams. The first was the Washington Senators. They were a replacement for the original Senators, who had moved to Minnesota and become the Twins. The second expansion franchise was the Los Angeles Angels. With their creation, the AL now had a team in California as well.

Entertainer and businessman Gene Autry headed the investment group that ran the team. The Angels played their first season at Wrigley Field—but not the one famously located in Chicago. The *other* Wrigley Field was in South Central Los Angeles. It was the longtime home of a minor league team that played in the Pacific Coast League.

BUILDING A TEAM

The Angels and Senators filled their rosters with picks from an expansion draft held in December 1960. The teams took turns choosing players made available by the other eight AL clubs. Naturally, teams protected their best players from being drafted. But the Angels did find a few diamonds in the rough.

Los Angeles picked Jim Fregosi with its 17th selection. The shortstop had been a minor leaguer for the Boston Red Sox. He was also just 19 years old when the 1961 season started. But Fregosi appeared in 11 games that year. By 1963 he was Los Angeles's starting shortstop. Over the next nine years, the

Jim Fregosi set team records for games played, hits, doubles, and triples before leaving the Angels in 1971.

line-drive hitter made six All-Star teams. He also won the Gold Glove Award for his fielding ability in 1967. The team eventually retired his No. 11 jersey.

The other surprise star from that draft was pitcher Dean Chance. The tall, sturdy right-hander was just 20 when the Angels called him up late in the 1961 season. The next year, he won 14 games and established himself as the team's ace. Chance's best season came in 1964, when he went 20–9 with a 1.65 earned run average (ERA). For his efforts, he won the Cy

Dean Chance had 11 shutouts in 35 starts during his Cy Young season of 1964.

Young Award, which was given to only one pitcher per year at the time.

Chance became good friends with his teammate Bo Belinsky. The colorful left-hander exploded onto the scene as a rookie in 1962, winning his first five starts. Among them was a no-hitter against the Baltimore Orioles.

Suddenly, Belinsky was a star, and he enjoyed the perks of being young, rich, and famous in a city known for its nightlife. Soon he and Chance were making headlines as they dated Hollywood actresses and frequented the city's hottest nightclubs.

A celebrity sighting was about the only way an Angel could get his name in the paper. The team finished third in the AL during its second season with an 86–76 record. But the Angels still couldn't get out of the Dodgers' shadow. While the Angels tried to improve, the Dodgers were the best team in baseball.

They won the World Series in 1963 and 1965 while featuring some of the game's top players.

It also didn't help the Angels that they were now playing in the Dodgers' stadium. The teams shared the sparkling ballpark the Dodgers built at Chavez Ravine when it opened in 1962. The Angels remained the number two team in town until their own ballpark in the southern suburbs was finished in 1966. More than 1.4 million fans came out to watch the renamed California Angels in Anaheim Stadium's first year. It was the highest attendance figure in the league, but California finished sixth in the AL that season. It would be a while before the Angels could put a winning team on the field.

THE SINGING COWBOY

Though few of the Angels' first players were household names, their owner was famous around the world. Gene Autry, "the Singing Cowboy," was the star of numerous movies, most of them Westerns. He also was a popular singer, writing and recording many hit records in the country music world. Autry also recorded a number of Christmas songs—including "Here Comes Santa Claus," "Rudolph the Red-Nosed Reindeer," and "Frosty the Snowman"—that remain holiday classics.

CHAPTER 2

PLAYOFFS AND PAIN

By 1971 Jim Fregosi had been with the Angels for parts of 11 seasons. He had frequently been California's best hitter. But in that time, the Angels had never finished higher than third place. The team's front office decided to trade Fregosi before the 1972 season. The New York Mets sent four players to California for the shortstop. One of them was fireballing right-hander Nolan Ryan.

The 6-foot-2-inch, 170-pound Texan was already an established pitcher. But with the Angels, the righty became a true star. Ryan finished 19–16 in his first season with the Angels. He led the majors with 329 strikeouts and nine shutouts. An intimidating presence on the mound, Ryan also

TRAGIC ENDING

Outfielder Lyman Bostock was hitting .296 in late September of 1978 when the Angels played a weekend series against the White Sox in Chicago. After the team's Saturday afternoon game, Bostock went to visit friends and family in his hometown of Gary, Indiana. That night, while out for a ride with his uncle, he was shot in a case of mistaken identity. Bostock died two months shy of his 28th birthday.

hit 10 batters and threw 18 wild pitches, most in the league. His wildness only helped him become one of the most feared pitchers in baseball.

In May 1973, Ryan tossed a no-hitter against the Kansas City Royals. It was the first of his career, but it would not be the last. In fact, it wasn't even the only one he threw that season. Ryan struck out 17 Detroit Tigers in another no-hit effort that July. By the end of the season, he had set an MLB record of 383 strikeouts for the year.

HELP WANTED

Ryan continued to excel as the 1970s moved along. With his "Ryan Express" fastball and an improved curveball, he threw a third no-hitter in 1974 and a fourth in 1975. That effort tied Los Angeles Dodgers great Sandy Koufax for the most ever.

However, the Angels still weren't winning. The team finished last in the AL West both years. Aside from lefty Frank Tanana, who led the AL with a 2.54 ERA in 1977, they hadn't had much success developing other pitchers.

California wasn't producing position players either. In the late 1970s, the Angels decided to start adding talent through free agency and trades. Before the 1977 season, they signed second baseman Bobby Grich and outfielders Don Baylor and Lyman Bostock. They also traded for catcher/outfielder Brian Downing.

That approach brought quick results. In 1978 the Angels fired manager Dave Garcia and brought Fregosi back to manage the team. They stayed in contention past Labor Day and finished 87–75, good for second place in the division. Before the next season, the Angels made the biggest splash of all, trading for Minnesota Twins first baseman Rod Carew. A seven-time AL batting champion, Carew was the AL MVP in 1977 when he hit .388. The Angels also traded for Twins right fielder Dan Ford. Those two proved to be the final pieces of the puzzle.

PLAYOFF DEBUT

In 1979 the Angels ran off 10 straight wins in early April to claim first place. They spent most of the season atop the division, eventually holding off the Kansas City Royals to win the West by three games. California led the AL in runs scored, getting contributions throughout the lineup. Downing finished third in the AL with a .326 batting average. Carew wasn't far

Rod Carew was one of many key additions to make the Angels a contender in the late 1970s.

behind him at .318. Ford drove in 101 runs. So did Grich, who also hit 30 homers. Baylor outdid them all. He blasted 36 homers, drove in 139 runs, and was named the AL MVP.

In the AL Championship Series (ALCS), the Angels faced the Baltimore Orioles, who had won 102 games to run away with the East Division. Game 1 featured a matchup of future Hall of Famers: Ryan against Baltimore's Jim Palmer. Each pitched well, and the game was tied 3–3 through nine innings. The Orioles won it on a pinch-hit three-run homer by John Lowenstein in the bottom of the 10th.

The Orioles jumped out to a 9–1 lead in Game 2, but the Angels fought back. Their late rally fell short when they left the bases loaded in the ninth, losing 9–8. Back in Anaheim for Game 3, the Orioles had a chance to sweep the series when they took a 3–2 lead into the bottom of the ninth. But again, the Angels rallied. Larry Harlow's walk-off run-scoring double gave them a 4–3 win. The momentum didn't carry over to the next game, however. Baltimore's Scott

Don Baylor led the AL in RBIs and runs scored during his 1979 MVP season.

Second baseman Bobby Grich was a key part of three Angels playoff teams in the late 1970s and 1980s.

McGregor shut out the Angels on six hits. The Orioles cruised to an 8–0 win.

ROLLER COASTER RIDE

The Angels hoped it was just the start of big things to come. But the 1980 season was a disaster. Ryan had left as a free agent in the offseason. The pitching staff fell apart without him. California used 13 different starting pitchers. The team ERA ballooned to 4.52, second worst in the major leagues. Numerous injuries hampered the starting lineup, and the Angels limped to a 65–95 record. When they got off to a slow start in 1981, Fregosi was fired and replaced by veteran manager Gene Mauch.

A few other big additions helped put the Angels over the top in 1982. Slugger Reggie Jackson had been one of baseball's brightest stars in the 1970s. His playoff heroics

Doug DeCinces finished third in 1982 AL MVP voting after hitting a career-high 30 homers.

with the Oakland Athletics and New York Yankees earned him the nickname "Mr. October." The 36-year-old showed he had plenty left in 1982 by hitting 39 homers and driving in 101 runs. Veteran catcher Bob Boone, a former Philadelphia Phillie, was a steadying presence behind the plate. The Angels traded Ford to the Orioles for third baseman Doug DeCinces. He responded with a career year, hitting .301 with 30 homers and 97 runs batted in (RBIs).

The Angels lineup was the oldest in baseball in 1982. Their youngest starting position player was 30-year-old center fielder Fred Lynn. The veterans were a perfect fit for Mauch's consistent, no-nonsense approach. The Angels won a franchise-record 93 games. A hot streak down the stretch allowed them to pull away from the Royals in the AL West.

SLIPPED AWAY

The Angels faced off with the slugging Milwaukee Brewers in the ALCS. The Brewers led the league in runs and home runs, so shutting down their power game would be key to the Angels. And through two games, that's just what happened. The Brewers hit just two home runs and scored five runs total as the Angels took the first two games in Anaheim.

However, the series then shifted to Wisconsin. The Brewers' bats woke up, and Milwaukee won the next two games to set up a winner-take-all Game 5. The Angels led 3–2 with two outs in the bottom of the seventh. Then Milwaukee's Cecil Cooper slashed a two-run single to left field, putting the Brewers on top. The Angels had a runner on second base with one out in the top of the ninth, but Downing and Carew both grounded out to end the game.

It was a crushing blow to the Angels, who had been one game away from advancing to their first World Series. Instead, they had to watch as Brewers fans stormed the field to celebrate their own inaugural trip to the Fall Classic. It was especially hard on the highly respected Mauch, who had managed 22 years before leading a team to the postseason.

Bob Boone won five Gold Gloves at the catcher position in seven seasons with California.

He resigned after the disappointing finish. Angels fans hoped the team was on the verge of a breakthrough. But there would be more drama to come before the club finally reached the promised land.

CHAPTER 3

AT LONG LAST

Gene Mauch decided to return to the Angels as manager in 1985. By then some of the team's veterans had moved on. But stars like Bob Boone, Doug DeCinces, Brian Downing, and Reggie Jackson remained. Mauch guided the Angels to 90 wins, but it wasn't enough to top the eventual World Series champion Kansas City Royals in the AL West.

A year later, California finished 92–70 and booked its spot back in the playoffs. The Angels had a solid offense, and they finally had the pitching to go with it. Two 25-year-old right-handers led the starting rotation. Mike Witt, a tall and lanky curveball specialist, won 18 games and posted a 2.84 ERA. And second-year starter Kirk McCaskill went 17–10.

Mauch also held on to a few trusted veterans. Right-hander Don Sutton won 15 games that year at age 41.

The ALCS opened in Boston against the AL East champion Red Sox. In Game 1, Boston's starter was AL MVP and Cy Young winner Roger Clemens. The Angels jumped on him for four early runs, and Witt coasted to an 8–1 win. Boston evened the series, but the Angels then won two straight in Anaheim, with Grich's RBI single in the 11th inning winning Game 4.

A REAL NAIL-BITER

That left the Angels and Mauch three chances to win one game for a trip to the team's first World Series. Game 5 was an epic that was talked about for years afterward. The Angels got home runs from Boone and Grich, and Witt allowed two runs through eight innings. Entering the ninth with a 5–2 lead, Mauch stuck with Witt. His closer, Donnie Moore, had blown eight saves already that year.

Witt got the first two outs, but he also gave up a two-run homer to former teammate Don Baylor. Mauch then turned to lefty Gary Lucas to face left-handed hitter Rich Gedman. Lucas hit Gedman with a pitch, putting the tying run on base. Mauch then called on Moore to face Red Sox center fielder Dave Henderson. The Boston slugger launched a home run to left field to give the Red Sox a 6–5 lead.

Manager Gene Mauch, *right,* and slugger Reggie Jackson, *center,* look on from the dugout during the 1986 ALCS.

However, the Angels weren't done. In the bottom of the ninth, Rob Wilfong's RBI single tied the game. Moore retired the side in the 10th. But in the 11th inning, he gave up a bases-loaded sacrifice fly to Henderson. That proved to be the game-winner as the series returned to Boston with the Red Sox celebrating a 7–6 win.

The Angels knew they'd thrown away their best chance to close out the series at home. They still had two opportunities to win the series, but the team never recovered from the collapse in Game 5. Boston routed California at Fenway Park. Game 6 was a 10–4 blowout. Game 7 was even worse, as Boston built a 7–0 lead after four innings. The final was 8–1.

BREAKING THROUGH

The Angels spent much of the next 15 years spinning their wheels. For most of the 1990s, they had two of the best left-handed starters in the game, Mark Langston and Chuck Finley. But the best the Angels could manage were second-place finishes in 1995, 1997, and 1998. Even though MLB had added wild-card teams in 1995, the Angels still weren't good enough to reach the playoffs any of those three years. The most notable event in that stretch was a slight name change. In 1997 the team started calling itself the Anaheim Angels after the city it played in.

In 2001 the Angels went 75–87 and finished 27 games out of a playoff spot. It was a 15th straight season without postseason baseball. Then, out of nowhere, the Angels broke through. The lineup hadn't changed, but the Angels won a franchise-record 99 games and earned a wild-card spot.

Hard-hitting third baseman Troy Glaus was the main power threat. He posted 30 homers

THE CALIFORNIA SPECTACULAR

The Angels also reworked their home stadium when they rebranded as the Anaheim Angels in 1997. The center-field seats were replaced by an outdoor scene built with artificial rocks but real trees. The "California Spectacular" also featured geysers that would cascade water down the structure.

and 111 RBIs while batting in the middle of the order. Three veteran outfielders also led the way. Smooth-swinging left fielder Garret Anderson led the team with 123 RBIs. Speedy Darin Erstad made all the plays in center. Right fielder Tim Salmon was a consistent clutch hitter who added 22 home runs.

Starting pitchers Ramón Ortiz, Jarrod Washburn, and Kevin Appier each won at least 14 games. Closer Troy Percival used his intimidating fastball to rack up 40 saves. Late in the season, the Angels called up 20-year-old Francisco Rodríguez. He arrived just in time to play a key role in the playoffs as Percival's setup man.

The Angels opened the postseason by shocking the New York Yankees, who had won five of the last six AL pennants. Then Anaheim beat the Minnesota Twins in the ALCS.

Troy Glaus hit 182 home runs over seven seasons with the Angels.

Francisco Rodríguez appeared in just five games during the 2002 regular season before winning five postseason games that same year.

Rodríguez and Percival were unhittable along the way. Rodríguez earned four victories out of the bullpen. His strikeout pitching earned him the nickname "K-Rod." Percival saved four of Anaheim's seven playoff wins. Finally, in their 42nd season, the Angels were about to play in their first World Series.

CALIFORNIA CLASH

The World Series was an all-California matchup between the Angels and the NL-champion San Francisco Giants. Behind sluggers Barry Bonds and Jeff Kent, the Giants had plenty of firepower. And the duo slugged a combined three homers in the first two games, both in Anaheim. After winning the first game, the Giants looked to be on their way to taking the second as well. However, Salmon helped avoid disaster with a tiebreaking home run in the eighth inning of Game 2. The 11–10 Angels win tied the series. The teams split two more games in San Francisco. But a 16–4 Giants blowout in Game 5 tilted the series in their favor heading back to Anaheim.

The crowd in Anaheim was louder than normal in Game 6. But the Giants didn't seem intimidated. They already had a 3–0 lead when Bonds went deep off Rodríguez in the sixth. An RBI single by Kent in the seventh upped the lead to 5–0.

The Angels were nearing another disappointing playoff defeat. But entering the bottom of the seventh, the stadium crew put the "Rally Monkey" on the scoreboard. A video of a monkey jumping up and down on the video screen had fired

Scott Spiezio's clutch three-run homer started the Angels' rally in Game 6 of the 2002 World Series.

up Angels fans all year. The players seemed to respond as well. The team had 43 come-from-behind wins in 2002.

The crowd went crazy, and the team answered the call once again. One-out singles from Glaus and designated hitter Brad Fullmer put two on for first baseman Scott Spiezio. On the eighth pitch of his at-bat, the switch-hitter cranked a home run to right field. Suddenly, it was 5–3.

Erstad led off the eighth with a homer. Salmon and Anderson followed with singles. Glaus capped the incredible comeback by blasting a double to give the Angels a 6–5 lead. Percival then retired the Giants in order in the ninth to send the series to Game 7.

ONE LAST RALLY

Angels manager Mike Scioscia turned to rookie right-hander John Lackey in Game 7. And once again, the Angels fell behind

1–0 in the second inning. But this time the Angels bounced back right away. Catcher Bengie Molina's RBI double tied the game in the bottom of the second.

That set the stage for the biggest hit of the series. Two singles and a hit batter loaded the bases for Anderson with no outs in the bottom of the third. The left-handed hitter cleared them by scorching a double down the right-field line. Erstad, Salmon, and shortstop David Eckstein all scored.

The Angels swarm closer Troy Percival, *center,* after the final out of the 2002 World Series.

Lackey did not allow another run through five innings. Righty Brendan Donnelly pitched two shutout innings. Rodríguez struck out the side in the eighth. Percival allowed two baserunners in the ninth before coaxing a fly ball to end the game. Erstad caught the final out. Salmon quickly embraced him. The rest of the Angels mobbed Percival. Four decades after the team's MLB debut, the Angels were finally champions.

CHAPTER 4

LEGENDARY TEAMMATES

Over the team's first four decades, the Angels had been called the Los Angeles Angels, the California Angels, and the Anaheim Angels. In 2005 the Angels made another slight adjustment. They changed their name to the Los Angeles Angels of Anaheim.

Whatever the name, the Angels were in the middle of the best stretch in team history. Slugging right fielder Vladimir Guerrero arrived as a free agent in 2004. He won the AL MVP Award and helped Los Angeles get back to the playoffs. But the team's run ended in the AL Division Series (ALDS) against the Boston Red Sox.

Vladimir Guerrero hit 39 home runs and had 126 RBIs during his MVP season of 2004.

MIKE SCIOSCIA

The most successful manager in Angels history was a longtime catcher for the Dodgers. Mike Scioscia spent 13 seasons with the Angels' crosstown rivals. He took over as manager in Anaheim in 2000 and lasted 19 seasons. He also managed Team USA's baseball squad at the 2020 Olympic Games in Tokyo, where it won a silver medal.

Over the next few years, the lineup changed as veterans moved on. Francisco Rodríguez became the team's closer in 2005. He led the league in saves three of the next four years, including a record 62 in 2008. Younger players like utilityman Chone Figgins and righty starter Jered Weaver took over larger roles.

However, the Angels could not repeat their success of 2002. In 2005 they reached the ALCS but lost in five games to the Chicago White Sox. Four years later, another ALCS loss came at the hands of the New York Yankees.

In 2010 the Angels finished with a losing record for the first time in seven years. The championship team was long gone. But Angels fans would soon have front-row seats to watch two of the best ever to play the game.

THE ROOKIE AND THE LEGEND

On July 8, 2011, the Angels called up a 19-year-old outfielder from their minor league system. Mike Trout was one of the

Mike Trout dives to make a catch during a 2012 game.

team's first-round picks in the 2009 MLB Draft. At 6 feet, 2 inches and 235 pounds, Trout looked like a football player. But he could do everything on a baseball diamond. He just needed to prove it.

After struggling during the rest of the 2011 season, Trout came back the next year ready to go. Few players in MLB history have possessed Trout's combination of power and speed. He put them both on display in 2012. He posted an

Albert Pujols tips his helmet to fans after tying Babe Ruth for fifth on the all-time RBI list in 2019.

MLB-best 49 stolen bases while also hitting 30 home runs. He was a consistent hitter too. During a seven-game road trip in mid-July, Trout picked up 14 hits. His batting average peaked at a scorching .357 before he finished at .326. That was good enough to earn him the AL Rookie of the Year award. He also came in second in AL MVP voting. It wasn't long before Trout was earning comparisons to some of the best players ever.

It helped that Trout was playing alongside one of those greats. The Angels signed former St. Louis Cardinals first baseman Albert Pujols in December 2011. Pujols was a former Rookie of the Year and a three-time NL MVP. His signing gave Trout a role model and mentor to follow early in his career, and the younger player didn't pass on the opportunity. "You've got to listen to him," Trout said of Pujols. "He's done everything in this game."

Trout increased his trophy count in 2014. First, his star shone bright at the MLB All-Star Game in Minneapolis. In the first inning, Trout drove a pitch off the right-field wall, raced around two bases, and slid headfirst into third with an RBI triple. Then, in the fifth inning, he doubled down the left-field line to drive in another run. For his efforts, he was named the All-Star Game's MVP. And at the end of the year, he also picked up his first AL MVP Award after leading the league in runs scored and RBIs.

Trout also got his first taste of playoff baseball that season. The Angels returned to the postseason after finishing 98–64. But it was a brief stay. Trout's only hit in 12 at-bats was a home run. The Angels scored only six total runs in a three-game sweep at the hands of the Kansas City Royals in the ALDS.

Trout added another All-Star Game MVP award in 2015 and was named AL MVP again in 2016 and 2019. But what he really wanted was postseason success. For that, he needed another star to join him.

DOUBLE TROUBLE

Shohei Ohtani arrived in Los Angeles from Japan in 2018. American baseball fans hadn't seen anyone like him since the days of Babe Ruth a century earlier. Ohtani starred in Japan as a right-handed pitcher and a left-handed slugger. He made his debut with the Nippon Ham Fighters in his home country at age 18. Soon his name was known in baseball circles around the world. After five seasons in his home country, Ohtani moved to MLB, choosing the Angels over six other teams. He burst onto the scene much the same as Trout, winning the AL Rookie of the Year award in 2018. At the plate, Ohtani had a .285 average with 22 homers and 61 RBIs in 104 games. On the mound, he went 4–2 and struck out more than one batter per inning in 10 starts.

Ohtani set new career highs of 46 home runs and 100 RBIs in 2021.

The only thing that held Ohtani back was injuries. A sore elbow hampered him throughout his rookie season. That led to major surgery that kept him off the mound in 2019, though he continued to hit well. On June 13, Ohtani became the first Japanese-born player to hit for the cycle in MLB. But his season was cut short by knee surgery in September. Another arm injury limited him to just two pitching appearances in 2020.

Ohtani celebrates after hitting a grand slam against the Tampa Bay Rays in a 2022 game.

Finally, in 2021, Ohtani put it all together and stayed healthy. He punished AL pitchers, hitting 46 home runs, 26 doubles, and a league-high eight triples. As a pitcher, he went 9–2 with a 3.18 ERA. Like Trout in 2014, Ohtani was named the All-Star Game MVP and the AL MVP. Team success was still hard to come by, however. The Angels finished in fourth place in the West in each of Ohtani's first four seasons.

When Los Angeles struggled again in 2022, there were rumors that Ohtani might be traded. But in the end he stayed with the Angels. The team hoped that keeping the two great players on board would eventually lead to another championship run.

TIMELINE

1961
The Los Angeles Angels debut as one of two new teams in the American League.

1964
Dean Chance finishes 20–9 with a 1.65 ERA to win the Cy Young Award.

1966
The Angels lead the AL in attendance during their first season at Anaheim Stadium.

1971
The Angels trade longtime shortstop Jim Fregosi to the New York Mets for Nolan Ryan.

1973
Ryan throws no-hitters against the Royals on May 15 in Kansas City and against the Tigers in Detroit on July 15.

1975
Ryan throws his fourth and final no-hitter for the Angels against the Orioles on June 1.

1979
Led by MVP Don Baylor, the Angels reach the postseason for the first time before losing to the Baltimore Orioles in the ALCS.

1982
The Angels win the AL West but fall to the Milwaukee Brewers in the ALCS.

1986
Despite being one strike away from advancing to the World Series, the Angels lose the ALCS to the Boston Red Sox.

1997
The Angels change their name from the California Angels to the Anaheim Angels.

2002
The Angels overcome a 3–2 deficit in the World Series to defeat the San Francisco Giants in seven games.

2004
Outfielder Vladimir Guerrero arrives as a free agent and wins the AL MVP Award in his first season with the Angels.

2009
The Angels make the playoffs for the sixth time in eight seasons but fall 4–2 in the ALCS to the Yankees.

2012
Trout is named AL Rookie of the Year after hitting 30 homers and stealing 49 bases.

2014
Trout is named MVP of the All-Star Game and wins the AL MVP Award as the Angels win the West.

2017
Japanese star Shohei Ohtani signs with the Angels in December.

2021
Ohtani makes history at the All-Star Game as the first player to pitch and hit leadoff. After the season he is named AL MVP.

TEAM FACTS

FRANCHISE HISTORY
Los Angeles Angels (1961–64, 2016–)
California Angels (1965–96)
Anaheim Angels (1997–2004)
Los Angeles Angels of Anaheim (2005–15)

WORLD SERIES CHAMPIONSHIPS
2002

KEY PLAYERS
Garret Anderson (1994–2008)
Don Baylor (1977–82)
Dean Chance (1961–66)
Doug DeCinces (1982–87)
Brian Downing (1978–90)
Chuck Finley (1986–99)
Jim Fregosi (1961–71)
Vladimir Guerrero (2004–09)
Shohei Ohtani (2018–)
Francisco Rodriguez (2002–08)
Nolan Ryan (1972–79)
Tim Salmon (1992–2006)
Frank Tanana (1973–80)
Mike Trout (2011–)
Mike Witt (1981–90)

KEY MANAGERS
Gene Mauch (1981–82, 1985–87)
Bill Rigney (1961–69)
Mike Scioscia (2000–18)

HOME STADIUMS
Wrigley Field (1961)
Dodger Stadium (1962–65)
Angel Stadium (1966–)
   Also known as:
   Anaheim Stadium (1966–97)
   Edison International Field (1998–2003)

TEAM TRIVIA

ON LOCATION

The Angels' original home, Wrigley Field, was frequently used as a location for films and television shows. In all, 31 films and shows used it as a backdrop. One of them was a 1951 movie entitled *Angels in the Outfield*. Despite the title, the film arrived more than a decade before the actual team. The film's plot takes place in Pittsburgh and centers on the Pirates. A 1994 remake did feature the Angels and was filmed at Anaheim Stadium.

CIRCLING THE BASES

Among his amazing feats, Mike Trout hit for the cycle in his first four All-Star Games. He singled in 2012, doubled in 2013, tripled (and had a double) in 2014, and homered in 2015.

MONKEY BUSINESS

The real monkey behind the Angels' "Rally Monkey" was a television star named Katie. She was most famous for her recurring role as one of the characters' pets on the sitcom *Friends*.

FANCY FEET

The Angels' second baseman from 1964 to 1969 was Bobby Knoop. Sportswriters nicknamed him "Nureyev" due to his exceptional fielding footwork. The nickname came from Rudolf Nureyev, who was a famous ballet dancer during the same time.

GLOSSARY

ace

A team's best starting pitcher.

bullpen

The area of a baseball field where relief pitchers warm up; also used to refer to a team's relievers as a group.

closer

A pitcher who comes in at the end of the game to secure a win for his team.

cycle

Hitting a single, a double, a triple, and a home run in the same game.

franchise

A professional sports team, including the top-level team and all minor league affiliates.

free agent

A player whose rights are not owned by any team.

no-hitter

A complete game in which a team does not allow any hits.

pennant

Another name for a league championship; in MLB, refers to winning either the American or National League.

shutout

A complete game in which a team allows no runs.

sweep

To win every game in a series.

utilityman

A member of a baseball team who plays various positions.

MORE INFORMATION

BOOKS

Flynn, Brendan. *The MLB Encyclopedia.* Minneapolis, MN: Abdo Publishing, 2022.

Gitlin, Marty. *Baseball: Underdog Stories.* Minneapolis, MN: Abdo Publishing, 2019.

Hewson, Anthony K. *GOATs of Baseball.* Minneapolis, MN: Abdo Publishing, 2022.

ONLINE RESOURCES

To learn more about the Los Angeles Angels, please visit **abdobooklinks.com** or scan this QR code. These links are routinely monitored and updated to provide the most current information available.

INDEX

Anderson, Garret, 27, 30–31
Appier, Kevin, 27
Autry, Gene, 8, 11

Baylor, Don, 15–16, 24
Belinsky, Bo, 10
Boone, Bob, 19, 23–24
Bostock, Lyman, 14, 15

Carew, Rod, 15–16, 20
Chance, Dean, 9–10

DeCinces, Doug, 19, 23
Donnelly, Brendan, 31
Downing, Brian, 15–16, 20, 23

Eckstein, David, 31
Erstad, Darin, 27, 30–31

Figgins, Chone, 34
Finley, Chuck, 26
Ford, Don, 15–16, 19
Fregosi, Jim, 8, 13, 15, 18

Garcia, Dave, 15
Glaus, Troy, 26, 30
Grich, Bobby, 15–16, 24
Guerrero, Vladimir, 33

Harlow, Larry, 17

Jackson, Reggie, 18, 23

Lackey, John, 30–31
Langston, Mark, 26
Lucas, Gary, 24
Lynn, Fred, 19

Mauch, Gene, 18–21, 23–24
McCaskill, Kirk, 23
Molina, Bengie, 31
Moore, Donnie, 24–25

Ohtani, Shohei, 5–6, 38–39, 41
Ortiz, Ramón, 27

Percival, Troy, 27–28, 30–31
Pujols, Albert, 37

Rodriguez, Francisco, 27–29, 31, 34
Ruth, Babe, 5, 7, 38
Ryan, Nolan, 13–14, 17–18

Salmon, Tim, 27, 29–31
Scioscia, Mike, 30, 34
Spiezio, Scott, 30
Sutton, Don, 24

Tanana, Frank, 14
Trout, Mike, 34–35, 37–38, 41

Washburn, Jarrod, 27
Weaver, Jered, 34
Wilfong, Rob, 25
Witt, Mike, 23–24

ABOUT THE AUTHOR

Patrick Donnelly is a freelance writer who lives in Minneapolis, Minnesota. He has covered Major League Baseball for more than 20 years.